D1714705

A *Lifetime*
of *Love*

"Coach Holtz has written a very personal and uplifting book about mutual love between husband and wife, their faith-life journey, and the raising of their family together. It contains insights and lessons to draw upon whether you are single, newly married, or married for decades. This helpful and inspiring book could be subtitled, 'How to succeed in marriage (and in life) by really trying.'"

Fr. E. William Beauchamp, CSC
Provincial Steward-Secretary
Congregation of Holy Cross,
United States Province of Priests and Brothers

"After twenty-five years of marriage and six kids, you start to think you know it all when it comes to life and kids, and then we read Lou Holtz's book! That kind of wisdom comes from a life well lived and lessons hard won. Readers will love his parenting honesty, be touched by his love for his late wife, Beth, and be inspired to 'recruit' (non-football types may call it 'court') their own spouses. *A Lifetime of Love* is one heck of a playbook for marriage and family life!"

Scott and Kathryn Whitaker
Secretariat Director of Stewardship, Development, and
Communications, Diocese of Austin; and
author of *Live Big, Love Bigger*

"Having worked for Coach Holtz in my college days I knew him to be an inspiring and amazing leader and teacher. I witnessed firsthand his love for his wife and family. Reading *A Lifetime of Love*, however, introduced me to a new side of Holtz. This book offers a deeper, softer, and more-transparent look into the sacrament behind the man. Filled with sincere and honest insight and timeless wisdom, Holtz draws on a life well lived and properly focused, giving all married couples (and couples-to-be) an invaluable guide to marital success. With his trademark wit and soul-rattling counsel, Coach Holtz has once again reveals what made him so successful on the field . . . namely his faith, focus, and family. This book is a winner and the couples who take it to heart will assuredly be victorious too!"

Mark Hart
Executive vice president of Life Teen International

"Inspiring! It is obvious that Coach Holtz and his lovely wife, Beth, approached their marriage and raising their children with the same devotion, passion, and preparation that Coach utilized to lead us as head coach for the Notre Dame football team. This book is a testament to the Holtzes' gift to rally and motivate people to approach marriage with trust, love, and commitment."

Shawn and Marcia Wooden
Former football player at the University of Notre Dame,
Miami Dolphins, and Chicago Bears; and
Global Real Estate Advisor at ONE Sotheby's International Realty

A Lifetime of Love

of Love

A Game Plan for Marriage
and Family Life

LOU HOLTZ

Ave Maria Press AVE Notre Dame, Indiana

© 2022 by Lou Holtz

Founded in 1865, Ave Maria Press is a ministry of the United States Province of Holy Cross.

www.avemariapress.com

Paperback: ISBN-13 978-1-64680-133-6

E-book: ISBN-13 978-1-64680-134-3

Cover and interior photos provided by the Holtz family. All rights reserved.

Cover and text design by Christopher D. Tobin.

Printed and bound in the United States of America.

Library of Congress Cataloging-in-Publication Data is available.

Contents

Introduction – ix

1
My Wife, Beth – 1

2
Appreciating Each Other – 29

3
Raising Children – 49

4
Staying Committed – 83

5
Till Death Do Us Part –103

Introduction

You might be asking yourself, "Why is Lou Holtz writing a book about marriage and raising children?" I've asked myself the same question, though I will point out that I have always said my greatest achievements in life are my marriage and my children.

For several years, my wife and I were approached by different book publishers about working together to write a book about marriage. I think many people were impressed by the length of our marriage. We were married for a total of fifty-nine years before my wife, the former Beth Barcus, passed away on June 30, 2020. Since then, I have felt obligated for the both of us to share some of our thoughts and ideas on marriage and raising children. I do not profess to be an expert on the subject of marriage or raising children. Neither did Beth. But I think in our life together we learned many lessons about what makes a successful marriage and how to ride the ups and downs of married life.

As for parenting, certainly if our four adult children and their wonderful families are the judges, we were successful in that area too. Their names are Luanne, Skip, Kevin, and Elizabeth. Each of them is married (collectively a total of 113 years at the end of 2020!) and, with their spouses, have raised wonderful families. In all of those years, not one of our children has had a marital problem, a financial problem, an employment problem, or a drug or alcohol problem. We have nine beautiful grandchildren, and by the time this book is published, we will have welcomed our first great-grandchild. I couldn't be prouder of my children, and I asked them and their spouses to add some of their own comments and reflections in this book.

Whether you have been married just a short time or many years as we were, I think you will learn some practical lessons on what it means to be a husband or a wife and a mother or a father through some of the remembrances from my life with my beloved wife. Likewise, if you are contemplating marriage either in the immediate or distant future, I think this book will present you with the realities and rewards of what it is like to be married.

Beth and Lou Holtz on their wedding day, July 22, 1961.

Chapter 1

My Wife, Beth

Beth Barcus and I grew up in East Liverpool, Ohio, a town that borders West Virginia and Pennsylvania on the Ohio River. East Liverpool was once the center for manufacturing ceramic toilets and other ceramic tablewares.

Whenever I would start dating a girl seriously, my mother would say, "Make sure you study her family. If she comes from a good, solid family, where marriage is truly cherished, then that will be her attitude as well."

I could not have imagined a better family than Beth's. Her parents weren't particularly fond of me at first, but I admired them. Eleanor, Beth's mother, was one of five children who had been raised singlehandedly by her mother, Grandma Czech, whose husband died early in their marriage. Beth's father, John "Bus" Barcus, worked in an automobile factory after serving in the navy during World War II. Eleanor and Bus had three daughters: Beth, Brenda, and Johanna. Beth was the oldest.

Bus and Eleanor bought a convenience store on the outskirts of East Liverpool. They were hard workers, and the store thrived. When I was coaching at North Carolina State, I would go home in the summers and work at the store myself as a change of pace. I have to tell you, it was the hardest job I have ever had. My children worked there too, picking up all the trash in the parking lot and keeping the store clean. They didn't necessarily appreciate the opportunity.

When they sold their store, I bought Beth's parents a home in Leigh Acres, Florida, near Fort Myers. At first, Eleanor hated retirement. She had worked all of her life, and she didn't know what to do with herself. She eventually learned to golf and made a lot of new friends. After Bus passed away, Eleanor came to live with us. Our children absolutely loved her.

My family was also very solid. When my father, Andrew, was away in the navy during World War II, my mother, Anne Marie, and I moved in with my grandparents in East Liverpool. Their last name was Tychonievich. My mother was the oldest of four siblings, the younger three being my uncles Bill, Walt, and Lou. My Uncle Lou was only ten years older than me. He was a high school football star, and I looked up to him until the day he died. He became my older brother, father, and best friend all rolled into one.

My dad had been in some of the most epic battles of World War II, including the Battle of Midway. I learned after he died that when the war ended, he was part of the troops preparing to invade Japan. Like many who returned from the war, the experience affected him in ways we didn't really know. He took a series of odd jobs when he returned; he worked on the railroad and drove a bus, for example. My parents seemed to have a happy marriage until I went away to college and my father left home. My parents never divorced or remarried, but that was a tragic part of my life. It was devastating for me in my late teens, for my older sister, Shirley, and especially for my younger sister, Vicky, who was around the age of ten. I can only imagine how such separations are hurtful in other families with younger children.

Beth was a beautiful, exceptionally popular girl at East Liverpool High School. I was very shy and timid, particularly when it came to the opposite sex. I never had a date in high school. I never went to the prom. I didn't know Beth in high school, even though her girlfriends ran around with a group of guys I was friends with.

It didn't look as if Beth and I would ever get to know each other. I went away to college at Kent State University and fell in love with another girl, but that relationship didn't work out. She ended up marrying one of my fraternity brothers.

Everyone thought Beth would marry her high school sweetheart, Ron Frese. But before that could happen, Beth went to live in Pittsburgh to study to become an x-ray technician.

Around this same time, I was about to go into the army to fulfill my military obligation. Before I left, I took a trip to New York City with three of my friends. We did all of the touristy things during the day, such as ride the subway, visit the Statue of Liberty, and climb to the top of the Empire State Building. At night, we went to see plays. I remember the *Music Man* and *My Fair Lady*. We stayed in New York for a week in a hotel near Times Square.

On the way home, we had to pass through Pittsburgh, and my friends told me they wanted to stop and see Beth. She and her roommates were having some sort of a party. A party in those days was when boys and girls would gather together with beer or soda and a pizza. There were no drugs or alcohol other than the beer. I had no desire to go to the party or to meet Beth, but my friends stopped anyway. Surprisingly, I had a great time that revolved around getting to know Beth.

Because I had a car, I was selected to run out for the pizza. I figured the group wanted me to pay for the pizza too. Beth agreed to ride along to show me how to get to the pizza parlor. This was the first time I had ever been alone with Beth, and I was amazed how comfortable she made me, a shy person, feel. She asked me about the plays I had attended in New York. I politely asked her how her boyfriend, Ron Frese, was doing, and she told me she was no longer dating him and that she was dating a doctor on a very casual basis. This gave me the courage to ask her to go on a date with me.

I remember our first date as if it was yesterday, or more to the point, I remember what I was thinking after the date ended. I said to myself, "I don't have any idea who I'll marry, but I know the one person who I will not marry is Beth Barcus!" Why? She had eye shadow on, wore dark hose, smoked one cigarette, and kissed me on the first date. But in fact, we really seemed to hit it off and went out on a date every night in the week before I had to leave for military service.

After I got out of the army, we continued to date and developed a great relationship. I knew I wanted to ask Beth to marry me, but I must admit the proposal was nothing very romantic. I never sought permission from Beth's father because I wasn't marrying him; I was marrying his daughter, and I didn't think he liked me anyway. The only thing that was important to me was that Beth would agree to marry me. The proposal really came about in our normal course of conversation. We talked about how we both wished to settle down and raise a family and what our desires and goals were for the future. I told her that I would like to spend the rest of my life with her, and she said she had no objections to that. We were engaged! Looking back, I do wish I would have proposed in a more special way, at least getting down on one knee. I will tell you that later in our marriage, when we visited the Holy Land and the site of Jesus's first miracle at the wedding at Cana, I did get down on my knee and ask Beth to marry me once again. This time she responded with an enthusiastic "Yes!"

After we decided we would get married, I tentatively accepted a job at Conneaut High School near Cleveland to teach history, be the backfield coach for the football team, and live happily ever after.

Then, at 9:00 p.m. on July 9, 1960, Beth told me she didn't want to marry me after all. She wanted to date her old boyfriend, Ron Frese.

That news was enough to make me want to get as far away from her and East Liverpool as I possibly could. I'd been offered a graduate assistant coaching position (rare in those days) with the football team at the University of Iowa because my college coach, Trevor Rees, was great friends with the Iowa head coach, Forest Evashevski. I originally turned down the graduate assistant position in order to stay home and marry Beth.

It took me exactly ninety minutes to pack up. I picked up my good friend Nevitt Stockdale, and we were on the road in my '52 Ford Fairlane to Iowa City, Iowa, by 10:30 that night. We drove all night to see if Coach Evashevski would still hire me. Somewhere out on the highway, Nevitt made a great observation. He said, "You and Beth have a love-hate relationship. You love her and she hates you." I didn't disagree at the time.

• • •

I spent the year at the University of Iowa. I worked in the hospital teaching physical education to disabled children and served as a full-time assistant coach with the football team. The team had a great year; we were fortunate enough to finish second in the county. I also completed my master's degree in arts and education. It was just a marvelous experience. I had no intention of returning home.

In the meantime, there were two updates from East Liverpool. First, Beth had moved home, and she and my mom were working together at the East Liverpool Hospital. My mom had taken a job as a nurse's aide, and Beth had been hired as an x-ray technician. And second, Beth had had another change of heart and broke it off one last time with Ron Frese. Beth wanted to reach me, and she kept after my mom to have me call her, which I did not. Finally, Beth called me herself. That was the era when women did not call men on the phone very often, so I was impressed that she did that.

I was facing other pressures from home. During the interval that Beth and I were broken up, I would take some of the new girls I was dating to visit my Uncle Lou, the closest male in my life, and my mother. Both of them had the same comments: "She's really nice" or "She is very attractive." But then they would add, "But she's no Beth." I kept putting off giving Beth an exact date when I would come home from Iowa, but I also realized I still loved her and was just trying to hide the disappointment of her breaking up with me.

Right before spring break, I was in the office with Coach Evashevski. He asked me if I was going home to patch things up with Beth. I told him, "No, Coach, I'm staying here. If it's meant to work out, it will." Coach Evashevski then said something that proved to be very meaningful: "Remember this: Absence to love is like air to fire. A little bit of air stimulates the fire. Too much air puts the fire out." Once he put it that way, I was on my way back to East Liverpool. It was during that spring-break week that we set our new wedding date: July 22, 1961.

• • •

By the time the wedding came around, I had accepted a full-time position at the College of William and Mary in Williamsburg, Virginia, as the offensive and defensive backfield coach. This was a great opportunity for me because William and

Mary played a very difficult football schedule in those days, and I was just twenty-four years old.

Our wedding was a whirlwind. I was in Iowa City until the day before, finishing up my comprehensive oral exam for my master's degree. And two days after the wedding, I had to be back in Williamsburg to entertain the guest speakers for the Virginia High School Coaches Clinic. (By the way, one of the guest speakers was Ohio State head coach Woody Hayes, and the other was his assistant Bo Schembechler, who would later be his rival at Michigan.) Because of all this, Beth made the arrangements for the wedding herself and would run all of her decisions by me later.

The wedding day was really the best day of my life. Not to say it was stress free. First, when I returned from Iowa, Beth told me she was going to have my dad take the wedding photos. "Beth," I said, "that will be a big mistake." Beth said not to worry because my dad had an expensive camera and other great equipment, which was true. The problem was he didn't know how to use any of it. And just as I predicted, not one wedding photo my dad took came out. Someone did send us a Polaroid shot of Beth, in her wedding dress, and me standing next to her. That's the only wedding-day photo we ever had.

At the time, the photo situation was the least of what Beth was worried about. The rehearsal for the wedding was set for Friday evening at St. Ann's Catholic Church in East Liverpool. But as she was leaving work at the local hospital to head over to the rehearsal, a lady in a Cadillac plowed right into Beth's sports car. There wasn't a great deal of damage, but Beth and the lady decided to exchange insurance information anyway. In fact, since they both had the same insurance agent, they decided to both go right over to his office to get it settled. Beth led the way, and the woman in the Cadillac followed. At a stoplight on an intersection with a hill, Beth's standard-shift sports car drifted back slightly into the lady's car and caused a second accident. The lady jumped out of her car and made a big scene trying to to tell what had happened. Beth was hysterical.

Meanwhile, the wedding rehearsal was to start at 5:00 p.m., but by 6:00, Beth's father still hadn't shown up. He owned a racehorse and was out at the track. The rehearsal started ninety minutes late. The rehearsal dinner was at my mom's house. She had relocated into a very small house as part of a duplex after she had separated from my dad. She made spaghetti, and her hospitality was truly special. Unfortunately, Nevitt Stockdale, who was to be in the wedding, went out to play basketball after the dinner and broke his leg. He couldn't be in the wedding. We dressed my cousin Billy in the tux we had rented for Nevitt, even though Billy was eight inches shorter.

On the morning of the wedding, my mother panicked when I went out to my first round of golf with friends and didn't get back to her house until 10:15. She thought I would be the one to be late for the 11:00 a.m. wedding. She was prone to panic. Despite all of this, I wasn't late, the wedding Mass went well, and so did the reception, which was held at the Knights of Columbus Hall. I do remember it was very hot.

Our plan was to begin our eight-hour drive to Williamsburg right from the reception. We left about 4:00 p.m., and I figured we would be in Breezewood, Pennsylvania, within three or four hours, where we could stop and spend our wedding night at a motel. We weren't in the car a half hour and Beth fell asleep. I guess she was exhausted from all the preparations. Plus she'd had a very difficult day before the wedding. I was getting tired too. When we reached Breezewood, every motel room was booked for the night. If you are a history buff, you might recognize that our wedding date, July 22, 1961, was also the centennial anniversary of the Battle of Bull Run, which happened in that region. There were thousands of people there to commemorate the event. Every motel from Breezewood to Williamsburg was booked. We didn't arrive to our new home until about 5:00 a.m. It was quite a start to our marriage.

• • •

Coaching at William and Mary and living in Williamsburg was really a great experience for both of us. Williamsburg is just a beautiful city. To prepare for Beth's arrival, I had rented a lovely little home. When Beth arrived, she did not like it all. Fortunately, our head coach, Milt Drewer, had just moved out of faculty housing and we were able to take over his apartment. It was centrally located, and Beth seemed to like it very much. We made many friends who remain our friends to this day. Everything seemed to be going well. Beth got work at the hospital as an x-ray technician, and I enjoyed working with the football staff at William and Mary. All in all, it was always a friendly atmosphere. Until one night when I did something I was not proud of.

One of our main social outings was to go to someone's house for dessert and to play bridge. On one of those occasions, we were at the home of Barry Fratkin, the sports information director at the college. I was an experienced bridge player from college; Beth was not. I was also very competitive. During the game, I told Beth out loud she had made a very dumb move with her cards. She responded, "If you say another negative thing, I am going home." Well, it was about two hands later when I made another comment, and she walked out of the house. I thought she was outside on the porch and would come back inside soon. She did not. I found Beth at home and apologized. I also made a vow that we would never play bridge together again. We kept that promise.

• • •

To be honest, Beth wasn't a great cook, but she was so fun to be around that I barely noticed. And I had learned my lesson after criticizing her bridge playing. It did take a little time to get used to each other's sense of humor. At first, I didn't think Beth even had a sense of humor. Or maybe my sense of humor was hard for her to understand. I know that in our first year of marriage she wrote me a little note telling me how much she loved me and how proud she was of me. I made a photocopy of the note and returned it with my message scrawled at the bottom: "Dear Madam, Thank you for your interest in me, but at the present time I am happily married and have no intention of pursuing another relationship. However, if the situation changes, I will certainly get in touch with you. Sincerely, Lou Holtz." I wanted her to think I received other notes similar to the one she wrote. Beth didn't think my response was very funny.

Eventually in our years together we came around to where our personalities and humor met more in the middle. At one point she told me she had made a decision that since she couldn't please everyone in the world, she would focus on only pleasing one person each day. She added, "Lou, today's not your day and tomorrow doesn't look very promising either." That was a funny thing for her to say, and I thoroughly enjoyed it! I kept bugging her: "How's the day after tomorrow look?" She would shake her head no and we would both laugh.

We didn't have an awful lot of money in those days. Someone gave us a card table as a wedding gift. We used that as our kitchen table. Apparently others noticed our financial situation. After my fraternity brother Rich Thompkins and his wife visited us in Williamsburg, he mailed a letter to all of our fraternity brothers that was forwarded by one of them to us. It read: "Please pray for the Holtzs. They are as poor as church mice." Well maybe we were, but we really didn't know it. What we did know is that we had made a commitment to each other that included the promise to stick things out whether rich or poor.

As time went on, we learned more about how different we were in other things besides humor.

For example, my wife's politics were very liberal and mine very conservative. One of our few arguments was over the infamous Kent State shooting in 1970. As a former ROTC member at Kent State, I took the side of the National Guard. My wife believed the students were mishandled by the soldiers. We agreed to disagree. What we did always share was our values and what we believed to be important for our relationship and in raising a family.

· · ·

While we were at William and Mary, our first child, Luanne, was born. At the time, there were no books on how to be a father (or how to be a husband, for that matter), and because my own dad was gone most of my formative years, I really had no background training. Beth was a wonderful mother right from the start.

Around the time we became parents, we both had the same thought: we had never been on a honeymoon. Beth worked some on-call shifts at the hospital on weekends, and I made some extra money from my army reserve obligations so that we could save up for a honeymoon. We were able to book a cruise from Fort Lauderdale to Nassau in the Bahamas for ninety-nine dollars each. Beth took Luanne to her mother's, and we were off for ten days. We stopped by the home of Bobby Bowden, the Florida State coach whom I met at William and Mary (and whose team I would coach against in the famous number one versus number two Florida State versus Notre Dame game in 1993, won by Notre Dame), and his wife, Ann. We were there for two days. I went to the office with Bobby during the day while Beth stayed at home with Ann and their five kids. The honeymoon was off to a rousing start.

When we finally got on the cruise ship, Beth discovered she had claustrophobia. I've maintained ever since that going on a cruise is an awful lot like being in prison, except that you have a chance to drown. Also, the regular piano player quit right before the cruise, and the young lady they brought in as a substitute could only play one song, "Yellow Bird," which was a hit by Arthur Lyman in the early sixties. "Yellow Bird" became "our" song for many years.

We ran out of money by the time we got to Nassau. Still, Beth said she needed to get me something to remind me of our honeymoon. She went to the local market and bought me a pipe and some tobacco for a total cost of fifty-six cents. I had never smoked a cigarette or a cigar before then or at any time since, nor had I smoked a pipe. I started smoking that pipe on the ship and continued smoking a pipe for the next fifty-nine years of our marriage.

Eventually I had a small room built in our house with extra ventilation. It was the only place Beth allowed me to smoke. She spent years trying to get me to give up the habit that began with her honeymoon gift. As I often said to her, "Beth, I don't drink to excess. I don't gamble, and I don't run around with other women. Now which of those other vices would you like me to take up to replace the pipe?" She said the pipe was fine.

• • •

After three wonderful years at William and Mary, we moved on to Connecticut and South Carolina and then, in 1968, to Columbus, Ohio, where I took the job of assistant football coach under Woody Hayes at Ohio State. It was a big step for my career. We won the national championship the season I was there. By this time, we also had three children. Being close enough to our home in East Liverpool, our family members, high-school friends, and college buddies were able to come out for every home game. It was a marvelous year, and we thoroughly enjoyed ourselves.

We were getting ready for spring practice to begin for the second season when, lo and behold, I got a call from William and Mary telling me that Marv Levy, the head football coach, had resigned to take a job in the NFL. They were offering me, at age thirty-two, the chance to become the youngest head coach in college football. It was a tough decision to leave Woody Hayes and the defending national champion team, but I took the job at William and Mary. In my second year, we won the Southern Conference Championship and played in the Tangerine Bowl against eleventh-ranked Toledo. We led the game at halftime but unfortunately couldn't hold on.

Woody Hayes noticed our success and asked me to come back to Ohio State for a visit the following summer. We now had four young children. We loaded them up in the car, along with the growing collection of cribs, diapers, and toys that came along with them, and drove to East Liverpool where we dropped them off at Beth's parents' house. Beth and I went on to meet with Woody Hayes. While at dinner, he offered me the position of assistant head football coach, defensive coordinator, and recruiting coordinator. More, he promised me that I would be his successor as head coach when he retired. The offer was both flattering and enticing. Beth very much wanted me to take it. She loved the experience we had before at Ohio State, living nearer to family and friends. It was a difficult decision. But we ultimately decided to remain at William and Mary. I thought that if I were to end up as the head coach at Ohio State, I wanted to earn the job, not inherit it.

One of the things that made my wife so great was that she was so supportive of my career. We talked over each move we made. Early in my career, when we were at the University of Connecticut and things weren't going so well, we sat down and talked about whether I should get out of coaching and go back to school to earn a doctorate or maybe go to law school. Those were the options. I listened to Beth when she told me she knew my heart was in coaching and that we should give ourselves five years in the coaching profession. If it hadn't worked out after five years, we would be young enough to move on to one of the other two options. We also agreed we would not evaluate our decision every year but wait until the five years were up.

Once we made a decision together, we both committed to it 100 percent. We tried to hold to the principle that any job change I made was in the best interest of the family for the long run. The decision to turn down Woody Hayes and remain at William and Mary for another season turned out to be the right decision, and one I do not regret one iota. In the five years after Connecticut, I had added coaching for a national championship team and becoming the youngest head coach in the country at a major college to my résumé.

• • •

In any career that requires numerous moves, it is never easy for the family, especially the children. For a head football coach, it's a relatively smooth transition to go to a new school. You put your name on the desk, and everybody's there wanting to know how they can help make you comfortable. My poor wife had to do much more. She had to find doctors for the children, get them settled in school, sell a house, buy a house, make new friends, locate shopping areas, and be a psychotherapist for the children who were leaving boyfriends or girlfriends. The list went on and on. I am so indebted to my wife for all she did for me and our family.

I'm not going to go into every different detail of every place we coached because it was always the same. Leave a home, friends, and experiences in one place and make a new home, friends, and experiences someplace else.

The purpose of this chapter was to tell you that sharing a life journey with someone you love and who has the same values and dreams as you do is simply irreplaceable. Your partner doesn't have to be exactly the same as you. You don't have to have the same background. One of you can be shy; the other can be outgoing. One of you can be outwardly beautiful and the other relatively plain. But if you share core values such as honesty, trust, and commitment to excellence, and if you truly love and care about each other, you will have a wonderful life together. That's what happened to me.

Beth and Lou Holtz

Chapter 2

Appreciating Each Other

When we made a commitment to write this book, Beth was to be by my side and contribute to it as well. However, because of her health, we never got around to starting work on this project. It was only after she passed away that I decided I'd try by myself, and with the help of our children, to keep our commitment and describe the lessons we learned being married. I am sorry my wife could not be here to share her comments in the book, but I am trying to express her thoughts as best I can.

I can honestly say that in all the things I've accomplished in this world, by far my greatest achievement revolves around Beth and the family we created. I was fortunate enough to be married to this beautiful woman for fifty-nine years.

By no stretch of the imagination do I pretend that I was the perfect husband. I knew from the start I would have to work at being a better spouse just like every other person who is in a marriage. It is not easy to balance family and career, but my priorities were always my faith first, my family second, and then football. Golf was up there too! I love golf, and became very active with it, probably spending too much time on the golf course when the children were young. I would tell Beth that God did not count the amount of time I spent on the golf course against my allotted time on this earth, so it would allow me to live longer. It made me feel good when I said it, and she would laugh, but we both knew it was not true.

• • •

We did reserve dedicated time to be together. We scheduled a Wednesday date night every week of the football season. We would go out to dinner and visit with each other. I would listen to her problems and concerns. I never allowed any problems

I had at the office to come home, but there were times when I would talk to her about the situations I was facing or decisions I had to make. Beth's opinions were always very important to me, and they would weigh heavily on me when I had to make a final football-related decision. I think she always knew that what she said to me was heard and valued. I think a wife appreciates a husband who is open and honest, and is not afraid to tell her about his own concerns and failures, knowing he is not looking for pity but rather for good advice and understanding.

Finances and keeping a budget are very important in a marriage. Some studies have shown most arguments and breakups in marriage are based on money. When we first got married, Beth had several thousand dollars in clothing bills and a large balance on a sports car. She wasn't accustomed to living on a budget and, at first, didn't adjust well to living on a budget after we established one, but she eventually became the manager of our finances.

I didn't make an awful lot of money at William and Mary, so it was necessary to set up a budget with all the important categories. First we paid ourselves by saving "X" amount each paycheck; then we would have an allotment each month for groceries, the car payment, the mortgage, clothing, furniture, and doctors. Then, when our car was paid off, for example, we continued to make that same payment we were spending on the car to the bank, so that the next time we bought a car, we could basically pay cash for it. We did the same thing with furniture and other household expenses. We had a very limited amount of money budgeted for miscellaneous expenses in our early years of marriage. I remember one time we debated whether to buy some peanuts we could snack on or Mitch Miller's record album. We finally decided on the album because we realized we could listen to Mitch Miller many times over, whereas the peanuts would be gone in a matter of minutes.

When you're on a budget, you have to base a decision not on what you want but what you can afford. As the years went along and our income grew, we got off the budget. Even then we tried to spend frugally. When I entertained an assistant coach, for example, by taking him out to dinner, my wife knew how I spent our money. Beth became one of the best money managers I know. She handled all of our investments, finances, and savings, and she did an outstanding job. She made sure that she arranged for our children to be in the best schools possible.

One of the things we wanted to do as grandparents was to set up an educational budget for all of our grandchildren. To this date, we've had grandchildren attend Notre Dame, Texas, Texas A&M, and St. Louis University. We have a grandson who played college football (at Texas), another who is a practicing attorney, and a third who studied aeronautical engineering. And that's just a small sample. We have two other grandchildren who are just embarking on their college careers. Beth, who had never lived on a budget before she was married, not only set up the grandchildren's educational budget but also was responsible for managing our charitable foundation.

Jesus said that much will be required of those who have been given much. We took his words to heart. Our foundation is the way we remained consistent with our giving. We had some causes that have been especially important to us. At Notre Dame, we gave to the Homeless Center of South Bend. In fact, our entire family volunteered there. We were also very involved in supporting pregnancy centers that support expectant mothers and their unborn children.

Whether it was in managing our family finances or our charitable foundation, Beth took the lead. Over the years, I had several investors and financial experts tell me that nobody could have set up our financial portfolio or manage our foundation any better than Beth did.

. . .

I always wanted to be home with Beth as much as possible. As a college football coach, this was a difficult wish to keep. Because I was gone nearly every night, especially during a season, we made an agreement around the third year of our marriage that if we were not together at 10:00 p.m. local time, I would call her if at all possible. We also made a pledge that if I wasn't able to call, we would each look at the clock at 10:00 p.m. and think about each other. That way we would always feel connected, even if apart for many hours. I also told Beth we could peek out the window and look at the same moon at the same time. That was another way we felt we were together when physically apart.

From Beth I learned to become a better husband. Very seldom did she ever say or do something that didn't make sense. At times I did or said dumb things. She was very patient with my stupidity.

And I think from me Beth did learn to become a better wife. That is the way it's supposed to work in a marriage. You learn from your spouse. You accommodate each other's needs. You build on each other's strengths and come to their aid in their weaknesses. Married couples make a commitment to each other, for better or worse, in sickness and health, and until one of you dies. But the commitment is also to each other's success and happiness.

• • •

I think Beth liked the fact that I continued to recruit her for fifty-nine years. (Maybe another husband would say "woo" or "court," but a football coach uses the term "recruit"!) I continued to open doors for her. I would tell her that she would get an electric shock if she ever put her hand on the car door handle. I opened doors for her when we were courting, and I did it throughout our marriage. It was my privilege to show her this sign of my respect and love for her. I always looked for sincere ways to praise her. I thought it was important that she knew how much I appreciated her, and also that I understood her challenges as a wife and mother in running the household. Whenever I had a chance, I would write my wife love notes from the office and then put them in the mail. She would be surprised a day or two later when the note arrived. I also left various other notes around the house—maybe in the laundry room or in a kitchen cupboard—telling her how much I appreciated the sacrifice she made for the family and how much harder and more important her chores were than mine. I was trying to win football games. She was trying to raise our children to be good citizens. I think you can understand why I thought her job was more important.

I don't want to make it seem as if I left all the household chores or tasks or raising children to my wife alone. Whenever possible, I helped her with chores around the house. Nothing helps a wife more than doing the dishes without being asked, unless it's mopping the floor, moving heavy things, or taking the garbage outside.

My regular obligation was to take care of the yard. We had a rule that the front yard belonged to Beth and me and the backyard belonged to the children. Our thought was that maybe one hundred people would come inside our house in the course of a year, but thousands of people would form an opinion of our family by the condition of the front of our home. We both considered neatness to be an important virtue. We felt that by keeping a neat yard, neat closet, and neat appearance of dress, it was saying that we were proud to be a member of our family. We passed this virtue onto our children as well. We told the children that the backyard was theirs to use and care for because it was their playground.

• • •

Beth certainly allowed me to follow my dreams, and she supported me at every step along the way. That is not to say she didn't voice her opinion if she felt we were headed in the wrong direction. We supported each other in our physical, spiritual, and moral needs. Beth accepted me for my frailties. I chose not to lift weights or to exercise a great deal but instead to focus on my profession. She accepted my choice to not win a Mr. Universe contest but to be a husband who would provide for her and our children, be caring, and be God fearing. I always strove to be a good provider and to give Beth all the necessities and luxuries I could afford. Some people will make more or less money than others, but anyone can try to make life for their spouse as easy and problem free as humanly possible. There will always be problems and difficulties, but these are easier to face when a husband and wife face them together.

I tried to support Beth in everything she did, whether it was with her Bible study group or her tennis game. I let her know I was there for her. When couples first get married, they both tend to put their best feet forward. Then they either fall off or stop altogether. I tried to never let that happen. I felt I was so fortunate to have someone like my wife, and I wasn't about to lose her. That's the reason I continued to "recruit" her throughout our years of marriage.

• • •

Beth herself was a very religious person. She converted to Catholicism two years before we got married and even before we started dating. Beth's family didn't go to any church when she was young. Not many girls went to church without their families in East Liverpool in those days, but boys did. Why? Because the local YMCA had a basketball league and each church had its own team. In order to play on a team, you had to go to Mass if you were Catholic, or Bible study or another worship service if you were Protestant.

I grew up praying traditional Catholic prayers, like the Rosary, which is a very special prayer. In fact, in my first year at Notre Dame, I met an alumnus who told me that she prayed the Rosary every day. If she had a special prayer request, she would offer a Rosary for the request and then say the Rosary for another thirty days of thanks. It so impressed me that I have prayed a daily Rosary ever since. Before Notre Dame's national championship game with West Virginia after the 1988 season, I prayed the Rosary thirty days before the game requesting that we win and thirty days afterward in thanksgiving for our victory. Beth never had those types of Catholic experiences growing up.

When Beth went to Pittsburgh to study for her x-ray technician degree, she roomed with Betty Lou Miley, who was and is a very devout Catholic. Beth was influenced by Betty Lou's devotion to her Catholic faith and converted while she was in Pittsburgh. I didn't know about any of this at the time, but what I found out later was that Beth became the best Catholic I ever knew. Her faith in God was much stronger than mine. When she was dying, she made me promise that I would continue to provide the necessary religious leadership for our children and grandchildren. I assured her that I would, and I could tell she was grateful even though by then she was so ill that she could not speak.

• • •

We went to Mass every Sunday, keeping our priorities in the order of God, family, football, and social activities. We prayed together for our family and with our family. When we prayed, we used the acronym ACTS. That is, we *acknowledged* God's greatness and the wonderful things he was doing in our life. We *confessed* our weaknesses and the things we were sorry for. The T is for *thanksgiving*, and we went from person to person with each one naming one blessing. Finally, we would *solicit* God for our needs. We would ask God to help lead us in the direction we should go.

• • •

Liz: Faith was important to my parents, and they encouraged us to participate in Young Life, the Fellowship of Christian Athletes, and church summer camps. After Sunday Mass we would go out to breakfast at the football facility and eat from the training table.

My mom used to pray for our spouses even before we met them. After being married to Mike for more than twenty-six years, I can say her prayers were answered. The importance my parents placed on faith shaped our parenting. Jesus Christ is the cornerstone of our family as well. I am grateful for my parents for nurturing our faith in God.

• • •

Mike (Liz's husband): Our marriage thrives because we share the same values. Faith and family come first. I know firsthand how important it is for us to raise, guide, and nurture our children with faith and strong values, just as my parents did for me and Liz's parents did for her.

. . .

Keeping this perspective in mind helped us when we were faced with special challenges. In 1991, just before Notre Dame played Michigan at home, my son Kevin, who has been a type 1 diabetic since age fourteen, went into a diabetic coma and was in the hospital for three days. Beth never left his side and neither did I. It was important for me to be there, to put my wife and son before football, and to let them know they were my top priority. When my family did not need me, then I returned to my football team. I considered the players on my team to be just like my own children. When I recruited an athlete, I promised his parents I would treat him just as I would my own son, and I tried to follow through with that. That didn't mean I was always going to shower my players or my own children with kindness and affection, because I was also responsible for teaching them to make good choices and directing them to discipline themselves. That is a father's and a coach's obligation.

KEVIN: I don't know if I realized it or truly understood as a teenager, but my mother and father showed me the importance of faith in living your life. They taught me that there are going to be both good days and bad days. The team may lose a game, but you realized the unconditional love and acceptance of God the Father was what was truly important and needed.

On the day my dad resigned as Arkansas coach, it was snowy, and my mother and I couldn't make it down the icy hill we lived on in Fayetteville to get to the press conference. Instead, we listened on the radio. I expected to hear the details of why he was leaving his job after taking the team to many bowl games. I did not hear any of that. I remember my dad read eight verses from Ecclesiastes 3. He quoted that "there is a time for everything and a season for every activity under heaven," and he concluded with "now it's time for me to resign as the head coach of the University of Arkansas."

I traveled a lot for my job and for various events. Obviously Beth's first priority was our children, and she couldn't go with me as often as I would have liked when I had speaking engagements. But I always wanted her to be with me at each football game. One of the things I negotiated into my contract when we went to Notre Dame was that she could travel with the team and partner on the itinerary with the team priest who had no wife. This was a foreign concept to the priests, and they weren't particularly enthralled with that idea, but they reconsidered and allowed Beth to be part of the travel party.

Beth started traveling to the away games when we were at Arkansas. I felt it was important to our players to realize she was part of my team and thereby their team as well. She was like a second mother for the players, and it was amazing how close many of the players felt to Beth. In addition, as the visiting team, we were usually invited to a social function put on by the opposing school before the game. I couldn't attend, but Beth could, and it gave her the opportunity to meet the wives of other coaches and to get out and socialize. After the game, I only wanted to be with Beth and my family. If we won, she didn't say a lot. If we lost, she didn't say a lot either. She listened to me express myself and share my feelings. Really, I was just thinking out loud, and she was there to hear me. I certainly needed her with me.

• • •

I often like to say that my wife was a saint and that I didn't pray for her, I prayed to her. For me, Beth was the source of the most spiritual support, especially after a game, whether we won or lost. I am certain that my wife is in heaven, and if for some reason she is not, then I absolutely have no chance of getting there myself.

The Holtz family, with Beth and Lou at center.

Chapter 3

Raising Children

We have four children, and as I like to say, "they're all girls but two." I can honestly say I would not take a million dollars for any of our four children. But if I was to be honest, I probably wouldn't take a million dollars to have had another one. Why? It's because I found out that I was only as happy as my saddest child, and the more children you have, the more difficult it is to avoid sadness. I know sadness is a part of life, and there can be growth from difficult times. But it is extremely hard for a parent to see their children in pain.

When we first got married and began to have children, some of the Dr. Spock and other parenting books were coming out, and we, like most others, had copies in our home. But really, we just sort of learned from how our parents had raised us and tried to emulate the things we liked and change the things they did that we felt were harmful to us as children.

When you have your first child, you worry about everything. By the time our youngest, Elizabeth, was born, she sort of raised herself. Our overall parenting desire was that we wanted all of our children to discover what they liked and what they were good at and then go and be themselves.

LUANNE: My parents encouraged each of us in our own individual talents and interests. We were always allowed to pursue activities of our choosing. But we were expected to try our best and not give up.

I always wanted to be a teacher. When I was little, I would offer the kids in our neighborhood pieces of candy in order to bribe them to be my "students." I remember collecting soda bottles in stadiums after football games and taking them to the grocery store to cash in for change to buy them the candy rewards.

I also created worksheets to use for my lessons. My dad would let me mimeograph them in his office, and I would give copies to all the kids who played school with me.

SKIP: Two of the lessons my parents taught me were (1) take responsibility for your own life, and (2) grow and learn from every experience. When I left the driveway to go away for college, my mom told me she was going to pray that I lived through all of my college experiences but, more importantly, that I learned from them. I feel her prayer to not only survive in this life but also to learn and grow from each new experience.

JENNIFER (SKIP'S WIFE): I am most impressed by my husband's ability to balance the demands of his job with his desire to be present in his relationship with me and our children. I believe the advice his mother gave him when he left for college made a profound impact.

What Beth and I emphasized with our kids the most was the importance of making good choices and, relatedly, accepting the consequences when you make bad choices. We believed that if we could teach our children some simple steps for making good choices, they would have lasting and meaningful success in life.

We also stressed to our kids that if they made bad choices, there would be ramifications.

As a parent, you have to be the supervisor of the consequences of those bad decisions. Some people call this "disciplining others," but my belief is that disciplining is not what you do *to* somebody but what you do *for* somebody. Disciplining is strictly a result of the choices a person makes. Choices determine everything that happens in your life. I've often said, if you choose to do drugs, drop out of school, join a gang, or get tattoos from head to bottom, you're choosing to have difficulty in life. And when you do, please don't blame me, because I didn't have anything to do with your choices! We tried to keep it simple and shared three basic rules with our children to help them make good choices.

SKIP: Dad had his rules, and we tried to live by them. We knew them well and knew they were not to be broken.

TERRY (LUANNE'S HUSBAND): It is very clear that Luanne relies on these simple rules she learned from her parents. As parents ourselves, we taught our children if they applied these simple rules in every aspect of their daily lives, they would be successful.

LUANNE: Unconditional love and discipline go hand in hand, especially during the teenage years. Establishing responsibilities and consequences for behavior not set forth by my parents helped me to learn boundaries and respect for my family and others.

To go along with our first rule, we taught them the difference between right and wrong. There are many sources for what is right and what is wrong. We used the Bible—especially the Ten Commandments—as a starting place. Worship God. Honor your parents and treat your siblings with respect. Don't lie. Don't steal. Be happy with who you are, and don't covet the life or things of others. Simply put, *do the right thing*. This was our first rule. We also taught them that the benefit of doing the right thing was that they would be able to build trust between their parents and among their siblings. Trust is something that would be essential for their other relationships, whether with teachers, employers, or eventually their spouses.

The second rule to help our children make good choices was to teach them *to do everything to the best of their ability*. Keeping this rule takes practice. We didn't start by demanding our children earn the best grades or be the best on a team. No, we began by encouraging them to make the right choices on smaller things, one choice at a time and one day at a time. Not everyone can be an All-American or on the honor roll or even the first string. Rather than choosing to be the "best student in class," we wanted them to do each day's daily school assignment to the best of their ability. Rather than automatically being the "best player on the team," we expected them to practice that day to the best of their ability. Even doing smaller, daily things to the best of your ability is not an automatic function. It is not magic. There are many temptations along the way to take an easier way out. We reminded our children that they will always have the freedom to make good choices or bad choices. Freedom is God's greatest gift.

The third and final rule we had for making the right choices had to do with helping to form our children's intentions. Of course, no one can control the intentions or motivations of another, but we strongly suggested to them that they take personal pride in what they do and *to make sure people know that they genuinely care*. We asked them to care about the tasks they were doing, the people around them, and themselves. This was the third rule.

KEVIN: Our rules could be summed up in the Golden Rule: "Treat others as you would like to be treated." We watched our parents live by this rule.

I feel that one of the most important things that happened to me in my childhood was having a paper route at age nine. I did not get to spend the money I earned. I didn't even save it in my own personal account. The money I earned went into the family budget. I felt a great sense of pride being able to contribute to our family in that way at that early age. I also learned about earning money and the costs associated with living. When our children were young and we would go out to breakfast, we found that the children ordered exorbitantly from the menu without any awareness of the check I was always picking up. In the early years of our marriage when we did not have a lot of money, we started a game whenever we went out to eat to give the children an idea of how much the meal cost and a little about our own family budget. I had them guess the total amount of the check. Whoever came closest would receive a dollar. We played that game for over thirty years, even when we took them out to dinner when we visited them at college. And the winner always got a dollar.

All of our children received work permits when they were fourteen years old and took jobs, mostly in the fast-food industry. We thought this was a good way to teach them more about making good choices. For example, there were plenty of choices built into work that involved doing the right thing. Would they keep their schedule? Would they follow all the directions of their supervisor?

Also, working was another way to teach them to do everything to the best of their ability. Our children were pleased when they received a commendation at work or even a slight raise to their hourly pay. Mainly, we wanted them to use their jobs as opportunities to be caring for others in the venue of customer service at a fast-food restaurant, where it isn't always easy to do so. Personally, I wanted them to see how mean the public can be to the person behind the counter so they would learn the life lesson of caring for others and treating them properly.

The jobs outside of our home were a natural extension of what we required of our children *at* home. All of our children had household chores, beginning when they were about two years old. Maybe it was to do nothing but put the spoons on the table for dinner, but everybody had something he or she was responsible for. On the refrigerator we fastened a chart with their names and chores they had for each day of the week. When they did their chore, they marked it off. We felt that everybody who lived under our roof was part of that household and that each person should contribute to the comfort of all of the family members.

LUANNE: Family was so important to my parents. They emphasized that contributing to family life will be a way that we will always stay loyal to one another.

Of course there were consequences for not doing a chore or not doing a chore to the best of their ability. As the children moved into their teen years, when one of them skipped a chore or didn't do a chore to the best of their ability, they were required to stay at home on Friday and Saturday nights. I remember walking past the rooms of whichever one of them was grounded for the night and would easily detect a bad mood. I'd say, "Why are you home on Friday night? I'd think you would want to be out having a great time. Oh, that's right, you chose to be here because you did not do your chores. Choices have ramifications. I hope you'll make a better choice next week!"

One time, Skip made a particularly bad choice when he was in high school. We told him the consequence of his bad choice was that he would not be permitted to drive the car for the next four months. After three months, my wife said to me, "I think we ought to back off. He's learned his lesson." I said if we wanted it to be for three months, we would have made it for three months. We made it four months without driving. When you give your word to your children, you certainly want to honor it, even when it becomes difficult.

Liz: One night I had a curfew. I think I was supposed to be in at 1:00 a.m. and I came in at 1:01. I opened the garage, and my dad was getting into his car. My mom had made him. He was going out to look for us, though I never figured out how he would find us. I asked him where he was going, and he said, "I'm going to the store." He was embarrassed that I had caught him going out to look for me. Now I know it was because my parents cared so much. Every time I would come in, he'd say, "Liz, are you home?" and I would say, "Yes, sir." He'd say "Night, I love you."

How can a parent make sure their children are making good choices? You can never be completely sure, of course, but you can observe and you can remain involved. We allowed our children to choose their own activities. They didn't do things that we wanted them to do. We wanted them to lead their own lives. But once they had chosen their activities, we monitored them and stayed involved.

LUANNE: My parents were always there for us, supporting us in our activities. When I wanted to change majors in college, I really wanted my father to give me his support. So I went into his office. We knew the door was always open to us. I told him that I wanted to change majors from education to social work. He sat there for a minute and then said, "Is that what you really want? Do you think that will make you happy? I only want you to do the best you can in whatever field you choose."

One thing we told our children was this: "You can make a decision once a year on what you're going to do. You want to play that sport? That's great, but you're going to stick with your decision for the entire year. I don't care if you are first string, last string, the coach likes you, the coach dislikes you. If you make that commitment to be on the team, you are going to keep that commitment until the season is finished." If one of the children didn't want to play the sport ever again after the season was completed, that was fine. But we also told them that if they weren't playing the sport the following year, they were going to be doing something healthy and beneficial. That meant we wouldn't allow them to spend their time indoors playing video games or watching television.

It was a bit complicated for me to keep track of how our children were doing. There were a lot of advantages of being a child of Lou Holtz. One memory that stands out was when I was coaching the New York Jets. Both of the boys worked at the practice sessions as ball boys. After one practice, held at Hofstra University, Skip was heading to the dining hall for lunch, and our famous quarterback Joe Namath drove up in his Cadillac and said, "Hop in and I'll drive you to the cafeteria." They walked in together, Joe took a look around, and said, "I really don't like the food here, and I bet you don't either. Let's go out to a restaurant and have a good lunch." Skip tells the story often about what a thrill that was and how nice Joe Namath was to him.

Another time, when I was coaching at North Carolina State, we played Houston in the Bluebonnet Bowl at the Astrodome, and the family got to participate in the bowl-game hoopla. It was an exciting game that went back and forth and ended in a 31–31 tie. What's remembered at our house about the game is that our son Kevin got on national television scavenging for coins in the stands. The announcers said something like "Lou Holtz's son is sure missing a good game!" As I said, there are many advantages of being the child of a college football coach!

But there were also many disadvantages too. Neighbors, teachers, and coaches placed many high expectations—sometimes unfairly—on our children. Also, I traveled a great deal out of necessity, due to coaching and speaking, and the kids and I missed one another whenever I was gone. There were times when my children resented my absence and would even complain. After the 1978 Orange Bowl game in which our Arkansas team defeated Oklahoma 31–6, the demands on my time became overwhelming.

My family wanted to know why I wasn't at my son's baseball game when he was playing shortstop with the new glove I had bought him.

My daughter wanted to know why I wasn't home when she went to the formal in her new dress. So one night when I was home, I gathered up the family and drove them to a neighborhood where children had many fewer material things than my children. I showed them the condition of the baseball diamonds and the schools and let them know that they were very fortunate to have the things they did. I wanted to let them know that their possessions and lifestyle came with a price: lots of hard work. Shortly after this, I happened to be home two nights in a row, and one of the kids said to me, "Don't you have to be somewhere, Dad? We don't want you to neglect your job." I assumed they had learned a lesson.

One of the smartest things we did was have all four children keep a diary while I was away. We asked them to keep a written daily record of what happened in school, at home, with their chores, and with their friends. They could write about anything else going on in their lives and in any style of their choosing. When I came home, I sat down individually with each child and had them go over the diary with me. We didn't do it all together because I wanted them to understand that they were each very special and I was really interested in what happened to them while I was away.

I always wished I could have been there each day to be with Beth and the children, but that was impossible. Their keeping of diaries while I was gone and our discussion afterward was my way of letting them know that I genuinely cared about them. We wanted our children to know that wherever their lives took them, whether it was the richest mansion on the block or even a cell in prison, we would always love them and be there for them.

Liz: My dad used to tell us: "If you get into trouble, my name will be in the paper. It will say 'five kids and Lou Holtz's daughter, "So I learned to be very careful and to do the right thing in public.

When our first child was born, Dr. George Olive gave me this great advice: "The most important thing a father can do for his children is to show them how much you love their mother." I never said a negative word to my wife or about my wife in front of our children. When your children know that you love their mother, it gives them a sense of security that you can't replace anywhere else. Remember, you can love a lot of people: your children, family, friends, fellow workers, and teammates. However, you can only be in love with one person. In my case, I was only in love with my wife, Beth.

Liz: Mike and I try to always make sure the kids know that we love and support each other. We try to make time to nurture our own relationship so we can be better spouses and parents.

No matter your profession, any parent will experience ups and downs in raising their children. Children themselves, especially today, face several cruelties that can bring them down. One of the most important things we discovered as parents was that we had to be able to lift up our children when things weren't going particularly well. Consequently, we came up with the idea of holding a "Praise Day" for a child who was discouraged, had a setback, or needed a lift. A couple of days in advance, we would designate an entire day of the week in that child's honor. We didn't do anything fancy. We let the child pick out the menu for dinner. After we ate, each sibling and then my wife and I would take turns saying nothing but positive things about the child being uplifted. The comments had to be positive, and they had to be sincere. I felt that really did an awful lot to help our children's self-image, particularly when they were down. Also, whenever one of our children had a birthday, we also gave a small present to the other children because we wanted them to look forward to their siblings' birthdays as well as their own.

LUANNE: When it was my turn for Praise Day, I always chose steak.

LIZ: And Skip always liked spaghetti. But no matter what we ate, we had to go around the table and say something nice about the person whose night it was.

KEVIN: I remember we had to say *two* positive things. No negatives. Sometimes we had trouble coming up with two!

SKIP: The comments had to be sincere, and we also had to give a gift.

LUANNE: We'd get a couple of small gifts.

LIZ: They weren't expensive, but they meant a lot.

SKIP: It was a neat thing. I remember getting homemade things. Liz would draw a picture for me.

LIZ: It was like having a birthday every six weeks.

SKIP: Praise Day was a day when we knew we were appreciated by the family.

KEVIN: It really made us feel needed and loved. I don't know any other families that did something like that. Maybe more should.

LIZ: After Mike and I got married, my parents gave us a special red plate. We use that red plate when our three children are together with us. Everyone has to go around the table and say something positive about the person who has the red plate. Over the years, a lot of love has been shared over the red plate.

When the children were really young, it was obvious to Beth and me that she was much closer to them because I traveled so much. So I initiated the "Big Buddy Club." Beth was not allowed to be in the Big Buddy Club. There were several perks of being a member to this club, such as going out for ice cream or for a game of bowling and different things along that line. We always looked for ways to celebrate the successes of our children and let them know they were special and loved. I think we did a good job. We wanted them to grow up with confidence and be proud of their accomplishments. In 1972, after my team at North Carolina State beat West Virginia in the Peach Bowl, I was fortunate enough to be honored by the Upper Ohio Valley Sports Club with a Man of the Year Award. Woody Hayes came up to present the award, which was very special to me. They gave me a huge trophy, and I came home and put it on our living room mantle. A couple years later, Skip made a Little League all-star team and received a small trophy. The first thing he did was come home, remove my trophy, and put his at the center of the mantle. We never bothered to change it back. We wanted to make sure our children understood that their trophies and achievements were as important as anyone else's, whether large or small.

• • •

As a coach, obviously we moved an awful lot, and that always presented a problem because we did not want to disrupt the lives of our children. I remember I thought about turning down one particular job because I felt it would be unfair to the children to have to give up their friends and the teams they were on, and start in new schools. Beth changed my mind. She said, "When the children are twenty-one, they can go live anywhere they want to live, but they aren't going to live their lives and ours too." It was a very uplifting comment for me.

Because we moved a great deal, the children got to know so many people that no one seemed a stranger to them. They learned how to meet new people, how to get along with people of a new region and culture, and basically how to adjust to the pace of everyday living they would face as adults. Having three siblings with them also made it a little easier. One of the smartest things I did, though, was to buy a trampoline. By the time the sun went down on the first night in our new home, every young child in the neighborhood was on the trampoline and became friends with my children. I always preferred that my children's friends come to our home rather than our children be someplace else. Consequently, whenever possible, we had a large recreation room and made sure our children knew that their friends were more than welcome there. We always seemed to have a large group of kids at our house, and we liked it that way.

Even when the children are right under your roof or nearby, there can be dangers. I believe in guardian angels, and the guardian angels of my children were kept quite busy. When we moved to Columbus for the Ohio State job, we bought a new home in a developing area. There was plenty of construction taking place, and most of the homes in the neighborhood were not finished. One evening in the summer, I came home, settled into my chair, and began to read the newspaper. My daughter Luanne leaned on an arm of the chair and said calmly, "Dad, do we have a ladder?" I told her we did not have a ladder and went back to reading the paper.

The more I thought about it, though, I wondered why she would need a ladder, and I asked Luanne to explain.

"I want to get Kevin," she answered.

"And where is Kevin?"

"He fell down the chimney of the house they are building next door!"

Poor Kevin. He had no skin from his belly button to his head, but he did not break a bone! His guardian angel must have softened the landing.

• • •

When Beth and I were growing up, most of our relatives lived in the same neighborhood. As parents, we became part of a generation that ushered in a more transient society. Consequently, in 1979, we decided we would commit to spending the first week of July that year and every year going forward together as a family. We picked the first week of July because that was convenient for me as a coach. We've chosen many places to visit and many different kinds of themes for our week together. We've gone to the mountains. We've gone to the ocean. We attended the 1996 Olympics together in Atlanta. We've even gone to a dude ranch!

One of the most memorable trips we took was when I was coaching at Notre Dame and we decided our family would go white water rafting on the Snake River in Wyoming. We also decided we were going to make this trip as luxurious as possible. We hired a guide, flew in to Boise, Idaho, and traveled in a van for three hours north to the Snake River. We would spend the first night at a motel before going white water rafting for the next five days. We would then spend the last night at the same motel before flying back to South Bend. Beth was not impressed with the motel. As a matter of fact, she would not even get out of her clothes and she slept on top of the bedspread.

The next day we were out on the Snake River. About fifteen minutes into the trip, the guide said, "Coach, you better button up, because we are getting ready to go through Big Chief." He said Big Chief was an example of class 5 rapids, one of the most difficult you could raft through. "Can you give me an example of class 6 rapids?" I asked him. "Niagara Falls," he answered.

I stuck my thumb down in that raft and held on as tightly as I could. We hit Big Chief, and I came out of the raft about three seconds before my right thumb. I had broken it in four different places, but at the time, that wasn't something I was worried about. I was stuck under the raft. I remember thinking when I was underwater that winning a national championship in football wasn't that important.

This trip was in June, and the weather for camping was brisk. After five nights camping, we stopped for one more night at the same motel we went to on the way in, and after spending those cold nights outside, even Beth had to admit the motel was marvelous. There was running water and television, and my wife was thrilled to be back in civilization. It's all about perspective.

As we were exchanging goodbyes at the airport, Kevin said, "Next year, let's do something less dangerous. Like running with the bulls in Pamplona!" We all got a laugh out of that.

• • •

Even now that our children are adults, we insist that everybody attends our first-week-in-July getaway, particularly if they wish to be in the will! I am happy to report that in thirty-three years, we haven't had many people miss. We also wanted the aunts and uncles to have time together to get to know their nieces and nephews and the cousins. Beth and I realized we wouldn't be here forever, and we thought it critical that all family members learn to care for one another.

Our format on family vacation is basically the same. In the morning, the men usually play golf while the women do a variety of things such as shop, go to the spa, or just visit with one another. In the afternoon we all spend time with the children (these days our grandchildren!). We share dinner together, with everyone chipping in with the preparation, and then we go out for a family activity such as bowling or miniature golf. At 9:00 every night we have a family meeting with prearranged topics. The first night it's our family business, and the second night's meeting covers the progress of our charitable foundation. We devote the third night to both prayer and discussing our spiritual growth and progress. On the fourth night, everyone—adults, teenagers, and children—gives an update on what has happened to them in the past year and what they expect for themselves in the year ahead. It is especially enlightening and fulfilling to hear the updates from our grandchildren! On the final night I meet separately with the men, and Beth would meet separately with the women. My talk is always a reminder of how men should love, respect, cherish, and treat women. I was never sure what Beth talked about, but my daughters informed me that their mom talked about proper ways for wives to treat their husbands, tips for raising children, and, of course, the importance of setting an example of prayer and practicing their faith. We have never had an argument or disagreement with a child, spouse, or grandchild about the format of the week or anything that would come up in the week that we shared together.

KELLY (KEVIN'S WIFE): Lou and Beth always put a high importance on us coming together for the family vacations. Marrying into the Holtz family was not for a lazy person. Our vacations are not just hanging on a beach with a book. Though there is some time to be still, our vacations to this day are filled with games of kickball, fishing, escape rooms, Wiffle ball, and lots of laughs.

Kevin has taken up where his parents left off. Whereas I might be content to just relax, read a book, or watch a movie on a Friday night, Kevin would rather we grab the kids and go bowling or play tennis together as a family. And guess what? I have never once regretted putting down a book or turning off the computer to go out and do some kind of activity with my husband and my kids.

One more piece of advice on parenting: it is important to never criticize your children, but you have an obligation as a parent or leader to criticize their performance. Please remember in raising children that when people need love and understanding the most, they usually deserve it the least, and what you say is important. Your tone of voice is important, and your facial expression is even more important. So, the madder you get, the softer you should speak and the more you should smile. I promise you that you will never regret this advice.

Lou and Beth Holtz with their grandchildren.

Chapter 4

Staying Committed

You may have heard of "lifetime contracts" in athletics. Some players sign large salary deals with their professional teams that seem to last well beyond the years they could possibly be effective players. There are also "lifetime contracts" in coaching. In effect, I signed one at the University of Minnesota when I accepted the head coaching position before the 1984 season. But I stayed only two years. Why? I also had a "Notre Dame clause" built into my contract. Like many Catholics, I had followed Notre Dame for most of my life. My grandfather was a Notre Dame fan. I marched to lunch, recess, and dismissal to the "Notre Dame Victory March" from third to eighth grades at St. Aloysius Grade School. I had a dream to coach at Notre Dame.

My "Notre Dame clause" in my Minnesota contract said that I could talk to the Notre Dame officials if the head coaching position ever opened up there. It did after Coach Gerry Faust struggled at Notre Dame (which I had hoped he wouldn't). I also realized that if we were successful at Minnesota, it would be logical that Notre Dame would come after me since the athletic director, Gene Corrigan, tried to hire me three different times when he was the athletic director at the University of Virginia. So, after praying on it, I had this stipulation put in my "lifetime contract" and was able to opt out and accept the Notre Dame job after the 1985 season.

The only lifetime contract I have really ever known was authentic is the one I made with my wife when we were married. The Sacrament of Matrimony is covenantal in nature—which is different than a contract—because it has been initiated by God. Because it is from God, it is *perpetual*. This means it will continue without interruption and last until the death of one partner. It is also exclusive. The bond of unity is between two married people. Their faithfulness and fidelity is to each other. No one else can come between them. Being faithful isn't always easy; it takes strength and determination to persevere and make marriage a lifelong commitment.

A problem with some couples today occurs when one or both forgets that once they join hands in matrimony, they have made the commitment to remain with their spouse for life, that is, until death does them part. Think of it this way: once you spin the wheel, it is not possible to back out of your bet.

• • •

Beth and I recited our marriage vows before God, and we took them seriously and sincerely. Vows of any kind can be hard to keep. Marriage vows can be particularly difficult. The person you marry at age twenty-four will not be the same person at age forty-four or sixty-four. But remember, neither will you. Is it worth it to persevere in keeping your vows? I absolutely believe it is. I don't care what you accomplish in this world, if you fail with your spouse and your children, then you've basically failed in life. This is just my belief.

There are several other challenges to keeping a marriage intact. There are job changes, which Beth and I were very familiar with. They can be challenging for everyone involved. When the University of Minnesota was recruiting me to be their head coach, I took my wife and my two youngest children, Kevin and Elizabeth, who were still living at home, to visit with the Minnesota officials and listen to the offer. They treated us very well while we were there, and they wanted us to make a decision before we left. They had provided a penthouse with several rooms for us to stay in. At first, we sat down together and tried to talk our way through the plusses and minuses of moving to Minnesota. Elizabeth was very concerned about leaving her friends. Kevin was about to go away to college, so his feelings were not as strong as hers. Beth and I didn't have a clear idea of what to do either. Finally, I said, "Let's go into different rooms and each spend thirty minutes praying that God leads us in the right direction." When we came out of our rooms, there was a peace and tranquility among the family and greater clarity in making our decision, and we agreed we should go to the University of Minnesota.

• • •

I think one of the common reasons a man or woman gives for why they want to divorce is "I deserve better." They go on to lament that they married a partner who was in great physical shape with goals and a high-paying job, and now the other person is overweight, out of work, and unmotivated. Beware: change is inevitable in marriage, and it may be one spouse's obligation to work with the imperfections of the other while recognizing that he or she is not perfect either. Fortunately, I never felt I deserved better than my wife, and thankfully

I don't think she did either. We were able to roll with the changes in our physical appearances and with other changes as well.

Spouses do change in other ways too—for example, emotionally and spiritually. Sometimes the sheer busyness of either person's schedule keeps them from connecting emotionally with each other for a period of time. If this emotional absence goes on for too long, a husband and wife may find that their relationship has gone stale, potentially to the point of no repair. That's why it's important to keep intentional ways of connecting each and every day and week in order to make each other feel special and needed. We always found it helpful to remember and talk over some of the great days from our past as well as look forward to the future as a way to stay connected.

A husband and wife will likely grow at different paces spiritually too. The early years of arranging for the children's religious instruction and sacramental preparation is over, and spouses have more time to delve deeper into spiritual topics and religious practices. When we were first married, we were the kind of Catholics who went to church and prayed as a family. We continued with those practices, but the older we got, the more we began to consciously rely on God for everything we did. We prayed over decisions big and small. We began to more publicly proclaim our faith. As I mentioned, Beth was the religious strength in our family.

When we moved to Lake Nona, near Orlando, Florida, in 1997, Beth developed a special relationship with a neighbor by the name of Dixie Keller. They walked together five miles every morning until Beth's health reduced the length of the walk to the point where she couldn't walk at all. While they were able to walk together, Beth and Dixie shared Bible verses and talked over their meaning. What a simple and effective way to share one's faith and grow spiritually! They were two ladies in the neighborhood who each felt she needed God in her life, and in each other they found a way to share it with someone else every day of the year. Beth and Dixie eventually started a Bible study group.

We had a prayer room in our home—blessed by Fr. Paul Henry, the rector of the Mary, Queen of the Universe Shrine in Orlando—and the group often met there. Later when she got sick, Beth often slept in her prayer room. She said it brought her peace. The Bible study group met every Tuesday. Eventually the group grew to twenty-four people from our neighborhood. The ladies had to cut it off at that number. I never bothered Beth on Monday nights, because I knew that Bible study was at 10:00 on Tuesday morning and she would spend Monday night reading, reflecting, and praying on the passages the group would be focused on for the week.

I have another piece of advice about the changes that naturally occur among spouses in a marriage: embrace them! Changes usually work out for the best. For example, Beth came into our marriage deathly afraid of dogs, and for good reason. When she was a young girl, a dog attacked her. She put up her arms and the dog bit a huge chunk of skin from the underside of her forearm. It left a permanent scar. Meanwhile, I had always grown up with dogs, and I hoped our children would be able to enjoy having a dog too. It took a long time for Beth to give in to her fears and accept a dog. It was a very courageous choice for her to try this new experience.

We eventually brought home Muffin, a miniature schnauzer, and we had her for several years. One day I came home from work, and Beth told me that Muffin had been diagnosed with cancer and the vet wanted to put her down. "What do you think?" Beth wanted to know. I said, "Well, I'm not vet, but when a doctor says to do something, I think it's wise to go along with the recommendation." Beth was so upset! Maybe as upset as I had ever seen her! She couldn't believe I would be so dismissive of Muffin. Beth prayed on what to do and told me the following day, "We are going to keep Muffin." The dog lived another five years.

Beth had changed from someone completely frightened by dogs to someone who loved our dog more than anyone else in the family did.

• • •

We thought it was a great help in keeping our wedding vows to renew them once a year. Sometimes we did it ourselves while attending a friend's or relative's wedding. In fact, I think a married couple should witness a wedding every year to remind them of their vows. (They should also attend a funeral once a year to remind them that they aren't going to be on this earth forever.) When Beth got sick, her weight was dropping at a rapid pace, and she was finding it hard to eat. I promised her that if she got her weight up to 110 pounds, I would take her to the Holy Land. I would have taken her anyway, but I wanted to give her some extra incentive. We were able to go to Jerusalem, and we stayed at the King David Hotel. We had a private tour of all the sacred sites. One of the places we went was Cana, the city where Jesus blessed the institution of marriage by performing his first miracle of turning water to wine. Beth and I renewed our own marriage vows that year at the Wedding Church at Cana, run by the Franciscans.

The virtue of trust has a great deal to do with remaining committed to your marriage vows. Really, you cannot have a productive relationship with anybody if it is not based on trust. But this is especially true in a relationship between a husband and wife. Trust between a couple is part of the falling-in-love process. It is during this stage of falling in love that more honest communication and personal revelation comes to the forefront. In order to trust, a person must reveal him- or herself to the other. This is difficult to do because there is always a concern that "if you really know me, you might not still love me—or even like me." But doing so is so important. Self-revelation involves sharing with the other all of your hopes and fears, good points and weaknesses. Only then can your partner know the real you and learn to trust you. The opposite of this self-revelation is to put on a mask and hide who you really are. Many people will put on masks when they are being inauthentic in their attempt to impress another. Unfortunately, some people even get married without knowing all about their spouse.

I wasn't as self-confident early in our marriage, and it affected the trust between us. Remember, I am not particularly handsome or well built, and I never had a date in high school. When classmates went to the prom, I was home playing with toy trucks. Consequently I wasn't a very confident individual. Early in our marriage, we were at a cocktail party and Beth was talking to another man, as any woman would do, and I found myself feeling jealous and low. I thought to myself, "Why wouldn't she rather be with him than with me? He is better looking, he's better built, and he's more intelligent than I am." On the way home, I unfairly criticized my wife for speaking with the other man. What was I doing? I was trying to diminish her self-image so it would be as low as mine. If I could do that, I thought, maybe she would think she was lucky to have me as a husband. My behavior because of my low self-confidence was not only hurtful but also damaging to the trust between us.

Beth and I made an agreement that we would have no secrets from each other, and we would try to never go to bed upset with each other. This helped our trust to grow. Self-revelation is an ongoing process in a marriage. If you don't let your spouse know your deepest thoughts, dreams, and feelings, it can lead to alienation.

Trust also goes hand in hand with freedom, which is God's great gift to us. Beth always granted me lots of latitude (for example, to be on the golf course with my friends and to go out for drinks afterward), and I made sure to never abuse it. Abuse of freedom leads to restrictions, which is why we have so many rules and regulations in society. I tried to repay that gift to my wife in many different ways. As I mentioned, Beth handled our finances, and I trusted her to manage our money, which she did well. I think for any couple embarking on marriage or any married couple having difficulty with maintaining trust in their relationship, each should first work on developing a mature relationship with him- or herself. The man and woman should each have and maintain trusting relationships with others—both other family members and friends. They should be able to offer and receive support as needed. Most importantly, they should be emotionally secure and not totally dependent on the other. While it's important to know as much as you can about your spouse before and during a marriage, it's even more important to know yourself.

I learned how much my wife trusted me shortly after attending a White House dinner to honor President Ronald Reagan. Beth and I were seated at different tables. She was seated next to Brit Hume, the television news correspondent. Brit told me later that he asked Beth, "Do you get nervous during a game?" Beth told him, "No, I know Lou is going to win. And if he doesn't, there will be a reason why." I felt good that my wife had that much trust in how well I did my job.

· · ·

I was awakened at about 2:30 in the morning on June 22, 2015, by the smoke alarms going off in our house. I tried to make it upstairs to grab my wallet, but the smoke was too intense. We were fortunate enough to make it outside. The fire probably started from a lightning strike. Our house burned to the ground. We lost everything—photos with presidents and the pope, a torch I carried for the 1996 Olympic Games in Atlanta, and several trophies. As we stood near the smoldering ashes at about 8:00 that morning, Beth was in tears. I told her, "We have until 8:00 tomorrow morning— that's twenty-four hours to cry and feel sorry for ourselves—but come tomorrow morning, we are going to move forward and we're not going to talk about what we've lost. The Lord put eyes in the front of our heads rather than the back so we can see where we're going rather than where we've been."

How much did I trust Beth? I gave her an unlimited budget to rebuild the house, and she exceeded it! Seriously, she built a beautiful new home. Her favorite feature was the prayer room. We realized even more that it is not possessions that make up a home or a life; it's the people. We were so fortunate to have survived the fire. As Beth completed the project of rebuilding our house, the words of a Catholic woman of the early twentieth century who is being considered for sainthood, Catherine de Hueck Doherty, came to mind. She wrote, "The oneness of marriage . . . the oneness of love in mind, heart, soul, and body, . . . the unbreakable bonds of an awesome sacrament: this is what will form a home. Home is not a dwelling built by hands. It is built by love. It is built by the unity of oneness that turns a veritable hovel into a palace of joy and peace." Certainly, aided by God, this was the home Beth had created for us.

• • •

There are many other things that can put stress on a marriage. A couple may not be able to have children naturally, or they may have a child who is ill and needs special attention. Sometimes children have behavior problems that cause strain in a marital relationship. We felt very fortunate that our children were able to make good choices in large matters and keep us from this type of pain. When the children leave the house, the so-called empty-nest syndrome brings about another dynamic. However, by cultivating a close relationship with your spouse apart from your children, a couple can avoid feeling lost when this occurs.

I've seen marriages where children dominate absolutely everything, and that's not good for a marriage. Yes, we have to give our children attention and make them part of what we do, but we have to continue to court and recruit our spouse as well. When people would ask what the secret to longevity in marriage is, I used to jokingly say that "it was our

children; neither one of us wanted custody of them."
But really nothing could be further from the truth.

· · ·

Many couples nowadays also have a double duty,
so to speak. They are caring not only for their own
children (and sometimes grandchildren) but also
for their own parents as they age. This can create
tensions, but it can also turn out to be a beneficial experience for everyone in the family. When
Beth's father died, her mother came to live with us
for about eight years. It can be trying when your
mother-in-law lives with you. Whenever things
became stuffy or tense between my mother-in-law
and me, I kept in mind what a wonderful daughter
she had raised. Looking back, I think about how
much joy she brought to our children when she
lived with us and how many good lessons she
taught them. My own parents, like Beth's, were
very special people. I remember something both
of them used to say: "We'll take care of you when
you are young. You take care of us when we are

old." The Bible has many passages that speak of caring for parents when they age. And the Fourth Commandment spells out that we should show respect and honor our older parents.

• • •

The marriage covenant is permanent. It is a binding agreement of love in which the man and the woman freely and irrevocably choose to love each other. Marriage is a commitment to love each other, care for each other, and remain with each other until one partner dies. We always felt there was no way out, so work it out! The first year I was married, we were young, and when we'd have a disagreement, I would say to my wife, "You go home to your mother." Her response to me was "No! You go home to your mother!" That was her attitude, and she was not going to let this marriage fail. I always wanted my players to have this same attitude of commitment to success. I wish more married couples would have this same attitude as well.

The Holtz family on their annual July vacation.

Chapter 5

Till Death Do Us Part

It was February 1997 when I took a call from Beth, and she told me her doctor had just informed her that she had throat cancer. It was squamous cell carcinoma, stage 4, and her doctor said he didn't think it was curable.

By the time Beth had reached home, I had already secured an appointment at the Mayo Clinic in Rochester, Minnesota. The doctors there confirmed the diagnosis and gave her only a few months to live. As with her determination in everything else, Beth lived another twenty-two years after being given that news.

They were not easy years for her. She had thirteen total hours of surgeries and eighty-three radiation treatments. The radiation destroyed her cancer and also her taste buds, saliva glands, and basically everything else associated with a healthy throat. Her health deteriorated over the years, and eventually she had to be fed by a feeding tube. She never complained.

• • •

Beth never liked to do interviews with the press. But she did one interview while she was sick because I asked her to, and it was only to answer one question: "What did you learn from having cancer?"

She answered, "I learned how much my family loved me."

The thing is, we didn't love her any more after she got sick than before. But it made me realize how important it is to let those we love know it each and every day we are with them.

• • •

The obligation of a spouse is to make sure the other person feels loved when you are around. Beth wanted me around when she was sick, and

I wanted to be with her. Without our love, I don't think either of us would have felt the same way. When Beth's health worsened, I offered to have a nurse with her twenty-four hours a day, seven days a week. She refused. She wanted me to be her caretaker. I was pleased to spend the time with her and care for her. I tried to attend each of her various doctor's appointments over the years. Eventually I had to help her get dressed and make adjustments with her feeding tube. I spent every spare moment with her. I wanted her to know I was with her.

• • •

In the hospital, about two days before she passed away, Beth's hands were quite swollen. The nurse said we should take her wedding ring off because it could cut off her circulation. Beth was unable to speak at that time, but she could still stare. She gazed right at me with eyes that could cut through steel. I knew she didn't want to take her ring off. The ring was so meaningful to her.

About one month after we were married, I told Beth, "I cannot wear a wedding ring. It feels so tight, and it really bothers me. Besides, I don't need a ring to remind me I am married to such a beautiful person." Beth was completely opposite. It was nineteen-karat gold. I paid $11 dollars for the ring, and she had never taken it off. If there was one thing I regret, it was having the ring taken off her finger even for a short time at the hospital. Another regret I have is that I don't have the ring with me to remember Beth by. We made sure she was buried with her ring on because she cherished wearing it, and we were sure that was something she would have wanted.

When Beth was in the hospital for the final time, I had every expectation that I would be bringing her home within a few days. The news went from "she'll be able to leave shortly" to "she's not going to make it" very quickly. She was on a ventilator, and we had already discussed her feelings about that. She had told me, "God determines when a person dies, not a machine."

When we decided to take her off the ventilator, Beth was brought into a special room that looked like a living room with a hospital bed in the middle. Three of our four children were able to arrive at the hospital and spend time alone with their mom before she died. They told me they spoke from their hearts and let her know in their own way how much they loved her. I spent those hours crying in sadness. When I was alone with Beth, I promised her one thing: I would continue to share the faith she had in God with her children and grandchildren and remind them to make prayer and the practice of their faith central to their lives.

We all gathered around Beth and were praying out loud when the staff came in to turn off the ventilator. They prepared us for what would happen. They said her breathing would get really heavy and then she would have scattered breaths for as much as two minutes apart. That is exactly what happened. I had never seen a person die before. The amazing part was that when Beth took her last breath, her spirit left her body. It was not the same radiant Beth. It was just a body, and her spirit had gone to the Lord.

• • •

Beth and I had spoken about her funeral, and it was planned very well. My good friend Digger Dawson owns a funeral home in East Liverpool. We have been close friends—and I mean close friends—since 1952. We had to get permission for Beth's body to be moved from Florida to East Liverpool. Another old friend, Bob Sebo, whom I played against in high school football, sent his airplane to Florida and returned Beth to East Liverpool. I was pleased she had one more trip to our hometown. Digger did a beautiful job preparing Beth's body and arranged for a funeral home to meet her in South Bend. Beth and I had purchased plots at the Cedar Grove Cemetery on the Notre

Dame campus years before. We would both be buried there.

Because of the pandemic, we were only able to have a brief time for the viewing and the guests had to be limited. Nevertheless, the occasion was very special and many people shared moving stories about Beth. After the viewing, my friends— including Scott Law, David Law, Raju Mantena, and Skip Strzelecki—went out for a glass of wine and a piece of pizza. We hadn't eaten all day. My friends promised me they would do everything to keep me occupied in the days and weeks to come. And that they did. In fact, they arranged for my closest friends to gather for a golf tournament. Scott chauffeured me to Michigan on his plane. I was very grateful for their friendship and support.

• • •

Beth's funeral Mass was at the Basilica of the Sacred Heart at Notre Dame. Fr. John Jenkins, the president of the university, was the main celebrant. The Mass was prayerful, moving, and beautiful.

My family and I decided I should not offer a eulogy given the emotional state I was in. Instead, Skip and Liz spoke at the funeral about their mother. Each did an unbelievable job. The one thing I did insist on was that one of the songs at the funeral be "Wind Beneath My Wings." For years after our honeymoon on the cruise, "our song" was "Yellow Bird," the only one the young pianist could play. Later on, we changed our song to "Wind Beneath My Wings" because that's how Beth thought of me and it was definitely the way I thought of her.

At Cedar Grove Cemetery, Fr. William Beauchamp officiated. This was special to me because Fr. Beauchamp was the vice president of athletics in ten of the eleven years I coached at Notre Dame. It was hard to leave the graveside, but I also knew Beth's spirit was not there. Her spirit was with God. The entire day was very beautiful. Fortunately we hired a professional videographer to tape everything from the viewing to the funeral to the graveside. Each of our children has a copy, and I am sure they will look at it from time to time, as I will. There is no way that you can prepare for the loss of someone you have spent fifty-nine years with, but you come to the realization that someday the grief you feel will turn to gratitude. Hopefully that next step is not far away.

• • •

A few months after Beth passed away, we were able to get the family together—children and grandchildren—for a family meeting. This was the first time we had been together since the funeral. I spent three hours telling them many things about their mother and grandmother that they had never heard before. I told them about Beth's parents, her early years in school, and some of the decisions we had to make as a family that they were not aware of. I was overwhelmed at the sense of gratitude I had for knowing Beth and being married to her for fifty-nine years. I reminded them of some of the sacrifices their mom had made for them and me, including some we had taken for granted. She had been a chauffeur, a maid, a cook, a nurse, a psychiatrist, and a friend. Really, the list could go on and on.

Beth saw the goodness in everyone. Whenever I said something negative about another person, she would immediately remind me not to pass judgment. "Only God can judge," she would say. Her love for God truly extended to her love for her neighbors. Beth belonged to a group called "Never Die Alone." She would receive calls in the middle of the night informing her that someone was dying and they had no one to be there with them. Even when she was sick herself, Beth would get out of bed to go be with the people she had never met just to make sure they would have someone nearby as their life was coming to an end.

• • •

My family and I shared many happy memories and things we hadn't thought about for years. I remembered how much Beth loved to serve liver for dinner. Liver was one of Beth's favorite foods, and I absolutely deplored it. Consequently, we made a deal that she would only have liver when I wasn't home. When I was traveling, the children felt as if they had liver every other meal. They came to me and complained. I spoke with Beth, and we made an agreement that the children would not receive liver for dinner more than once every six weeks. Of course, the children marked on the kitchen calendar the days they were served liver and tried to keep their mom to the agreement.

I also asked each and every one of them what they would do in the future to honor Beth. The consensus was that they were going to honor her by living as she did as a loving spouse, caring parent, faithful Christian, and beautiful light to the world. I promised to do the same.

• • •

There was a time I felt Beth would love me more only for whatever I accomplished professionally or financially. On December 3, 2020, I received the Presidential Medal of Freedom from President

Donald Trump. It was the only breathtaking moment I ever had in my life without my wife. The president said some very nice things in his speech about Beth, including describing my wife as a "strong and good person" and pointing out that she was "looking down at me with incredible pride." While both kind statements are no doubt true, I had realized long before this day that Beth truly loved me for who I am and not for what I did or how much money I made. It feels so good to know that about a person you are married to.

Lou Holtz is a Hall of Fame college football coach who served as the head football coach at the University of Notre Dame from 1985 to 1996, leading the Fighting Irish to the consensus national championship in 1988.

He is also a popular motivational speaker and an author of several books, including the *New York Times* bestselling *The Fighting Spirit* about Notre Dame's 1988 championship season, his autobiography *Wins, Losses, and Lessons*, *A Teen's Game Plan for Life*, and *Three Rules for Living a Good Life*. After leaving coaching, Holtz became a college football analyst for ESPN until retiring in 2015.

Holtz has received numerous honorary doctorate degrees and has received a number of honors not only for coaching but also for his philanthropy. He was inducted into the College Football Hall of Fame in 2008.

Holtz and his late wife, Beth, have four grown children, nine grandchildren, and one great-grandchild. He lives in Orlando, Florida.